For

The Silent Soldier

Jane Swift

Copyright © 2024 Jane Swift

All rights reserved

The characters and events portrayed in this book are fictitious. Any similarity to real persons, living or dead, is coincidental and not intended by the author.

No part of this book may be reproduced, or stored in a retrieval system, or transmitted in any form or by any means, electronic, mechanical, photocopying, recording, or otherwise, without express written permission of the publisher.

ISBN: 9798883096180

Cover illustration by: Kelly Jeffs

For my family

CONTENTS

	Page		Page
Chapter 1	1	Chapter 14	73
Chapter 2	5	Chapter 15	79
Chapter 3	9	Chapter 16	85
Chapter 4	15	Chapter 17	91
Chapter 5	21	Chapter 18	97
Chapter 6	29	Chapter 19	101
Chapter 7	37	Chapter 20	105
Chapter 8	43	Chapter 21	111
Chapter 9	47	Chapter 22	117
Chapter 10	53	Chapter 23	123
Chapter 11	57	Chapter 24	127
Chapter 12	61	Chapter 25	131
Chapter 13	67		

Chapter 1

"It came upon the midnight clear, That glorious song of old, From angels bending near the earth, To touch their harps of gold."

The carol singers stood outside the front door of Pollywiggle Farm, their breath making white clouds in front of them in the frosty moonlit evening, scarves wrapped snug around necks and hats pulled down over ears. Donald and Martha Fairweather stood at the open door with their grandparents, listening as the voices rose and fell in the clear crisp country air.

A bright full moon shone in the sky, looking twice its usual size. It was surrounded by a beautiful white halo tinged with pearly pink and glowing gold, the sky's own Christmas light decorations. "There'll be a sharp frost tonight" Grandpa had predicted earlier when he'd come in from shutting up the horses, stamping his feet and blowing into his hands to get warm. "You might want to go to bed with a hat on, keep them little lugs covered up" he joked, gently flicking Martha's earlobe with his chilly fingers as he passed her.

Martha had giggled. She had been toasty warm and comfortable, sitting right up against the kitchen range in the tattered old armchair; the most favoured seat in the house, despite its frayed cushions and worn arms. With a squashy feather cushion behind her back, her slippered feet on the colourful rag rug, and Henry, the great ginger tomcat on her lap ("a kingly name for a kingly cat" her Granny always said), Martha hadn't wanted to move at first when the doorbell rang.

"Up you get" her Granny had gently chided, when the door had been opened to the carol singers, and as Martha stood there now, listening to the beautiful words of the old carol she was pleased she had. The singers came to a close and the family all clapped enthusiastically. Granny reached into her deep apron pocket. "Thaa's marvellous" she exclaimed as she dropped a couple of coins into the collection tin. "I feel as though Christmas has really begun now." She closed the door and they hurried back to the warmth of the kitchen, where the air was filled with the scent of stew and dumplings, and the cat was purring at having got the chair all to himself.

Much earlier that day, Martha and Donald had caught the train from London to Norfolk, their suitcases stowed on the luggage racks, the window on the door to the carriage slid right down so that they could wave to their mother who was standing on the platform at Kings Cross. It was so early that it was still dark, and the gas lamps cast soft light across her pretty face, framed by her fashionable cloche hat and fur stole. "See you in five days!" she'd called to them. "On Christmas Eve! It won't be long my darlings" and then the guard had blown the whistle, the fires were stoked, and the train billowed steam as it picked up speed, the children leaning out of their window to keep waving until they'd rounded the corner.

They hadn't ever caught the train on their own before, but now that Martha was ten, and Donald deemed to be a sensible boy of eight, their parents had asked the train conductor to keep an eye on them and had let them travel on a few days ahead, now that school had finished for the holidays. They were going to spend Christmas in

Norfolk with their grandparents and they couldn't wait. Met at the station by Jack the farm hand, in his horse and cart, they rode in the back with their suitcases at their feet and blankets across their knees. They hadn't minded the cold as they bumped along the country lanes, as they were so excited to get to Pollywiggle Farm. Past fields and hedges, the flat landscape stretching out either side of them and the sky extending over their heads, somehow so much bigger and more magnificent than it felt in the city. "There's the church!" Donald shouted as they rode into Little Billingham. "And the river" joined in Martha. "We're nearly there!"

Granny had spotted Jack approaching and had come to the yard, wiping her floury hands on her apron as they clattered to a stop, and then enveloping the children in a huge bear hug. "You must be worn to a ravelling" she said, "and just look at these sooty faces! Let's get you cleaned up and ready for tea."

Chapter 2

Ellen Fairweather, the children's granny, was not unlike the cottage loaf she was in the middle of making. A small woman, she was pleasantly plump, warm and homely. Having floured and kneaded the dough, she placed it on a tray, covered it with a damp tea towel, and left the bread to prove before baking. Her rosy cheeks and rough hands told of the hard-working life she led, but she was always ready with a smile which reached all the way to her twinkling blue eyes and the recipient of that smile couldn't help but beam back. Her white hair was worn pulled into a bun at the back of her head, covered by a bonnet when she left the house, and she was rarely seen without her long apron tied over her skirts.

Granny was a kind, comforting sort of a person, the sort you felt safe with, especially when enclosed in one of her warm hugs. She smelt of face powder and Cussons soap, and although her embraces were soft, her arms were strong. Martha had recently had a growth spurt, and was now almost as tall as her grandmother, yet despite her small stature Granny had an air of authority and there was no question as to who was in charge in the house.

She was fair and open-minded, but she could also be stern, especially about manners and respect, and she expected things to be kept clean and orderly. Martha remembered one visit when she had left the milk jug on the kitchen table after breakfast, instead of returning it to the cool shelves of the pantry, and the milk had soured in the sun. "There's a place for everything, and everything in its place" Granny had told her, quite sharply. "Mind you remember that from now on, I can't abide waste." The spoiled milk was mixed in with the pigs' slop, so it wasn't completely wasted – nothing was on the farm – and Martha had helped to carry the pail of slops out to the pigs when Grandpa went to see to them, to make amends.

Next to Granny, Grandpa looked like a giant. He was six foot in his socks, taller in his work boots, and a big man with it. He had a broad chest, tanned muscular arms from the physical nature of his work, and was still lean and healthy and working just as hard as ever despite his advancing years. He wore a flat cap on his head and his trousers were held up with braces over a shirt in the winter or a white vest in the summer. When the children were little he used to swing them up onto his shoulders, or bounce them on his lap. They squealed with delight as they were bumped from knee to knee, safe in the knowledge that his big hands held them gently and he would never let them fall.

Bert Fairweather could read the vast East Anglian skies, the subtle changes in cloud, colour and temperature, and knew as well as the animals when there would be rain coming, or an overnight frost. He loved the animals on his farm, and as he went about his daily jobs he'd talk to all of them: the cattle and the pigs, the Norfolk black turkeys and the chickens in the yard, but he'd linger a little longer with his favourites, the Suffolk Punch horses. Big heavy working horses, they had powerful shoulders and a willingness to work that made them perfect for tilling and harvesting. Despite their size they had a gentle temperament, so although they towered over the children, Martha and Donald also loved spending time with them, brushing their beautiful chestnut coats until they shined, and stroking their velvety noses.

The farming day started early, before daybreak in the winter, and most of Grandpa's day was spent outside, regardless of the weather. He would break three times a day: for elevenses, dinner (often taken to him by Granny), and tea or 'fourses' at 4pm. In the summer months he'd carry on working again after tea, but in the winter as the dark encroached and the chickens huddled together in their roosts, the family also hunkered down, perhaps playing a game of cards by the light of the paraffin lamp, before giving in to weariness and making their way to bed. "Early to bed, early to rise" Granny would say as she made hot water bottles. "Makes a man healthy, wealthy and wise" the children would finish, reciting the saying that had always been part of their bedtime routine at Pollywiggle Farm.

Chapter 3

When Donald woke in the morning, for a moment he couldn't think where he was, but then it all came rushing back to him. The long train journey to Norfolk, the cart ride, the carol singers. He wriggled further down inside his bed contentedly, the top sheet protecting him from a scratchy blanket (both still securely tucked around him), and on top of that, the heavy quilted feather eiderdown. He felt as snug as a mouse in its nest and thinking this, curled himself into a little ball, pulling the covers up over his nose too.

A sudden rush of cold air hit him as his blankets were rudely pulled back. "Come on sleepy head, let's get up!" said Martha, poking him in the ribs. "Quick, up you hop, we can get dressed in the kitchen" and she dashed out of the bedroom door, carrying her clothes in her arms. There was no point staying in bed now, so Donald swung his legs out, reached for his pile of clothes which he had laid out ready the night before, and quickly followed his sister through the cold house down the stairs.

In the kitchen, they flung their clothes out across the top of the range and over the rail at the front, hopping from foot to foot, the backs of their legs pressed against the warmth of the old stove. Granny laughed. "Come along you pair of jumping jacks, pull those things on, and have some breakfast" and while warmed socks were pulled over tingling toes, she poured steaming tea from the big brown pot, catching the leaves in the tea strainer that was placed over the top of the mugs.

"Grandpa's been out for a couple of hours already" she said "and it's Monday wash day today, so I don't want you getting under my feet. The whites are already boiling in the laundry copper, and I'll be up to my arms in suds all day, so you'll need to take yourselves off." Martha and Donald glanced at each other and grinned. A day exploring without any grownups sounded like heaven to them.

After breakfast they laced on their boots, pulled on their coats and gloves, popped an apple each into their pockets and set off from the farm.

"Where shall we go first?" asked Martha. "To the river? Or to see the horses?"

"Let's go to the wood" replied Donald. "We haven't ever explored there on our own before."

The frost crunched under their feet and the winter sun shone bright above their heads as they stepped purposefully over frozen ridges in the ploughed field towards the line of trees at the edge of the farmland.

The ancient woodland was magical in the frosty winter morning. The sunlight filtered down through silver birch, rowan and beech, making ice crystals on the frozen ground sparkle and glint. There were fallen trees to clamber over, dens to be discovered beneath low hanging branches, and at one point they spotted a deer in the distance through the tree trunks, standing proud in the dappled light, before leaping gracefully away and disappearing once more.

The berries were bright on the holly bushes, a vivid scarlet against the glossy green leaves, and a robin alighted on one of the branches, unwittingly creating a perfect Christmas card scene. "Look Martha!" whispered

Donald, inching nearer to the little bird who was fluffed up against the cold. "Look how close I am!" He reached out a finger, ever so slowly, but the robin opened its wings and flitted away to the next bush.

Donald followed, pushing past prickly holly, and laughing as the robin darted forward again, this time to perch on an alder tree, its leafless branches adorned with small brown cones. "Let's see where it's taking us!" Donald called, and the children followed the robin through the wood, his red breast leading the way. All of a sudden, they emerged from the undergrowth, and found themselves on a narrow single track, at the end of which was a house. Built from red Norfolk brick, with bottle green wooden window frames and sills, it was solid and sturdy, and yet had a mysterious air: quiet and dark, with no smoke rising from the chimney on this chilly day.

"Who do you think lives here, in the middle of the wood?" said Martha, her voice hushed, as the air around them seemed to still. There was no sign of the robin anymore, and the only sound was the hushing of the trees, and the crunch and rustle of frosty leaves beneath their feet.

"I think we should go back" whispered Donald, anxiously.

"Don't be such a baby" Martha retorted, feeling cross with herself for being scared too, and not wanting it to show. "It's only a silly old house, let's go and take a look" and she strode towards it, with Donald reluctantly following behind.

The low sun hung behind the house, and the windows looked dark. Martha started to feel more confident out of the shadowy sighings of the wood as they approached the quiet building. No animals announced their arrival, no dog barking or horse whinnying.

"It must be deserted" she said, advancing on the house, and then, just to frighten her little brother, adding "Maybe a witch used to live here, but she's flown away to join her coven" and she turned to Donald, raising her hands into claws and cackling.

Donald stood stock still, his pink cheeks draining of colour, his eyes widening.

"What's the matter?" laughed Martha "haven't you ever seen a witch before?" but the noise of a door slamming made her whirl round, as a fierce old woman dressed all in black emerged from the house, a cane raised in her right hand. "Off with you!" she cried "Nosying around my house!" and she shook her cane. Martha backed away, reaching for Donald's hand. "I'm sorry, I - I'm sorry" she stuttered "We didn't know…" and as their hands found each other they turned and ran back to the safety of the wood and their grandparent's farmland beyond; but not before they'd glimpsed a pale face at the upstairs window, gazing out at them, one hand pressed against the glass.

Chapter 4

Almost back at the farmhouse, the children slowed their pace, breathing heavily from their dash through the woods. "Did you see that?" gasped Martha "The face at the window?" Donald nodded, panting heavily. They had stopped shaking and now that they were back on familiar territory were growing angry at having been shouted at. "Who was that horrible old lady?" asked Donald. "She didn't need to frighten us, we weren't doing anything wrong!" "I'm going to ask Granny" replied Martha, "she'll know." But when they got back, Granny was still busy with the washing in the scullery, red faced and harassed from hours of scrubbing and rinsing clothes, then feeding them through the mangle which was hot and heavy work. "Here, come and make yourselves useful" she called, passing a basket of white sheets to Martha. "Hang these on the line in the yard, the frost will help to keep them white."

When the washing was finally finished, the scullery

cleaned and damp clothes hung above and around the range in the kitchen to dry overnight, it was time for the weekly bath. Grandpa lifted down the tin bath from its nail on the wall, placed it in front of the range and filled it with the laundry water which was still hot from the dwindling fire. Granny opened out a folded screen to give the bather some privacy and the cleanest (Martha) went in first, followed by Donald, then Granny and finally the grubbiest (Grandpa) going last.

It was teatime before the children got a chance to tell their grandparents about their day. A simple meal of bread and cold meat since there had been no time to cook, a slice of fruit cake, and a warming cup of cocoa. The four of them sat around the scrubbed pine kitchen table, muscles aching from the days' work and adventures, bodies gently relaxing with the joint comforts of warmth and nourishment. The morning's events seemed so far removed from this contented scene that Donald began to doubt it had even happened.

"I had to break the ice on the pigs' troughs this mornin'" Grandpa told them. "I reckon we might get snow before the week is out." He looked at their tired faces. "What did you two get up to?"

"We went exploring in the woods" Martha began, and as the fright of their encounter in the woods washed over Donald once more, he interrupted, his voice growing faster and more high pitched as he went along. "We saw a robin, and we followed it and it took us to a path" he gabbled in a great rush. "And there was a house. It was scary. We thought there was no-one there, but there was. An old witch shouted at us. And we didn't even do anything wrong!" he finished in a crescendo of injustice.

"Slow you down" Granny said soothingly. "Begin at the beginning and go on from there." So between them Martha and Donald described their encounter with the woman in the woods, and the face at the window. "Who lives there? Do you know them?" Martha asked.

"That we do" replied Grandpa with a sigh. "Thaa's old Mary Ostler. She's a rummun' and no mistake. Do you reckon they're old enough to hear the tale?" he asked, turning to his wife. Granny nodded and so Grandpa continued.

"That house used to be a place of joy once upon a time.

Oliver and Connie Butters and their son Sam lived there together. The house is set back in the woods, a little way from the village, but that's how they liked it, quiet and secluded, away from the hustle and bustle. They grew flowers and kept chickens, Connie was always singing, and Sam was a great one on the piano, playing all the popular songs. Then of course the war came. Oliver signed up, and Sam followed him just as soon as he was old enough. Connie didn't want him to, he was only a boy, but what could be done?" Grandpa paused and Granny placed her hand on top of his.

"Well, word came that Oliver had been killed. Of course, Connie was distraught and so her sister Mary Ostler, who has no family of her own, moved in, to be of comfort to her. But then, not long after, a telegram arrived to say that Connie's only child, young Sam, was missing in action, presumed killed. Poor Connie couldn't take the grief of living without her son as well as her husband. She gave up on life I'm sorry to say, and despite Mary nursing her, Connie couldn't carry on."

"That's so sad," said Martha. "Is that what's made Miss Ostler so cross with everyone do you think?"

"That's not all of it" said Granny, picking up the story. "After the war ended, one cold day, not unlike this one, Mary hears a knocking on the door. She goes to answer it, and who should be standing there but Sam Butters: her nephew, Connie's son. He'd been reported missing after a battle, but miraculously had survived and he had returned home."

"He int the boy he used to be though" Grandpa added sadly. "He must have seen some terrible things I reckon. And to come home to find both his parents had died, well, that proved too much for the boy. He can't, or won't, talk anymore. That old house has gone from one filled with music and laughter to a silent sad shell of a home."

"He doesn't go out" Granny explained. "Mary likes to keep him safe at home, away from prying eyes. They've become very reclusive. Do you know what that means? They keep themselves to themselves. I used to visit now and again, take up a bag of spuds or a bunch of daffodils when Connie was still there, but Mary doesn't like anyone going near her house now and who are we to meddle?"

Later that night as Martha and Donald lay tucked in their beds, watching the glowing embers in the little fireplace that heated their bedroom, they talked about Sam the silent soldier in the house in the woods. Martha looked across at her brother, his eyes and nose peeking out from under the eiderdown.

"He must be ever so lonely. Imagine never going out or seeing anyone other than your aunt."

"And a horrible aunt at that - a witch! She's keeping him locked up there, all by himself."

"Well, that's not entirely true. You heard Granny and Grandpa; Mary's keeping him safe, it sounds as though he must be terribly unhappy."

Martha rested her head back comfortably into the feather pillows and as she lay quietly an idea crept into her mind, of going to visit Sam, to talk to him and make friends with him. Tiredness stole across her, limbs and eyelids growing heavy, and she drifted into sleep where she dreamt of soldiers and witches, and dark wintry forests.

Chapter 5

Pollywiggle Farm had been in the Fairweather family for generations. Passed down from one Albert Fairweather to the next, Grandpa's father Old Albert had passed on his skills and knowledge to his eldest son Bert, and in turn, Bert taught his own son Al over the years how to plant seeds and nurture their growth, clip a chicken's wing so that it didn't fly away, care for a herd of cattle, turn a field, balance the books.

Martha had never really given much thought as to why her father didn't work on the farm, until a couple of years ago when they had been visiting and she'd overheard the grown-ups talking. It had been one of those warm spring days where the promise of summer stretches ahead and they'd carried the kitchen table out to the garden to enjoy the sun. Lunch consisted of fresh bread, cured ham, apples and cheese. Grandpa ate this sort of meal the way he always did, whether sitting on a wall at the edge of a field or at the table with plates: he took out his pocket knife, pulled open the blade and used the point to spear a piece of cheese and bring it to his bread. He also used the knife to cut slices of apple, his thumb guiding the blade through the fruit. The children watched in awe as he effortlessly sliced and speared, marvelling at how he didn't cut his thumb off!

After an unusually leisurely lunch, Donald wanted to go to the pond to see the tadpoles. The large pond was full of reeds and lily pads, a few fish, and at this time of year hundreds of wriggling black tadpoles that had emerged from the thick slicks of frogspawn. It was an exciting place for a little boy but too dangerous for him to go on his own, and so he was encouraged to stay on the lawn in sight of the grown-ups while they let their lunch go down. He was soon distracted by a line of ants, and watched as they marched purposefully through the grass. Grandpa went back to work, and Martha's mother Emily carried the dishes inside to the kitchen.

Meanwhile Martha had climbed the apple tree and found a comfortable crook in the branches in which she now lay languidly below the arc of the cloudless blue sky. A fat bee, laden with pollen, buzzed from blossom to

blossom, and a bright red spotted bishy barnabee*
scuttled along the branch and onto her outstretched
finger. She felt happily full and lazy as she felt the
warmth of the spring sun on her face and listened to the
soothing sounds of the buzzing bee and the murmur of
adult voices below.

Her father's voice suddenly broke through her reverie,
and Martha's ears pricked up. "You have to stop asking
me" he was saying in a tight voice which Martha hadn't
heard before. "I'm not coming back and that's that. How
am I supposed to run the farm with one leg?" Martha
peered down through the apple blossom to see her
daddy gesturing to his prosthetic limb, fitted after he lost
his left leg in the Great War. "I can barely manage the
walk to my office, I'd be no help here whatsoever and
would be a spare part, a burden to you."

"That's not true" Granny replied, placing her hand over
her son's, but he pulled it away angrily. "You could get a
job in the village and the children could learn about the
farm - "

a ladybird in Norfolk dialect

"What job?" he retorted, his voice rising. "What job Ma? There are no jobs for injured men like me. I'm extremely lucky to have the one I have, and it's a good job too. I wish you could be proud of me, I wish I could work here on the farm, but I can't. I wish I was the man I used to be, but I'm not." He put his hands to his face and Martha saw his back shudder as he drew in a deep breath.

She sat very still in the branches of the tree, not daring to move. They must have forgotten that she was there, and she didn't want to be noticed now, they might think she'd been eavesdropping.

"We are proud of you," Granny said, her voice catching a little, as though she was trying not to cry. "We are so proud of you. We only wish we could see more of you and Emily and the children. And that we could know what will happen to the farm. Your dad's not getting any younger, we have to think about the future."

"I know Ma" Al replied, his voice softer again. "But things have changed. The war changed everything. I'm so fortunate to have a job, to have met a woman who wanted me despite all this" he signalled at his leg again, "and to have made a life for ourselves in London. It's not the way we thought it would be, but the world has changed, and we have to change with it. I came back from the war, so many men didn't… we have to be thankful for what we have." He took another deep breath, and began "I suppose – " but then hesitated, glancing quickly at his mother and then away again, as though afraid to say the next words. "I suppose we will need to look for a buyer for the farm at some point."

"That int right though" Granny retorted querulously. "What about Donald? To keep Pollywiggle in the Fairweather family?"

"We live in London! And Don's only a boy! How is that going to happen Ma? I don't see that it can." He pushed himself up from the table impatiently, holding on to the edge as he found his balance on the uneven grass. "Look, we're going round in circles here. Let's leave it for now. Come on Donald!" he called, "Let's go and see how those tadpoles are getting on."

He hobbled over to Donald and Granny watched as they headed towards the pond together, then she rose from the table too and walked slowly towards the house. With no worry now of being discovered, Martha shifted her position in the tree and let out a shaky breath. She had never considered before what would happen to the farm when Granny and Grandpa became too old to run it; she hadn't even contemplated the fact that they were getting older. They were simply Granny and Grandpa. They'd always been there and she had naively thought they always would. It dawned on her now that of course they wouldn't be around for ever, and that thought made her feel that she'd been silly and immature which in turn made her feel cross. Her eyes pricked with tears and she swiped her hand across her face to wipe them away.

She also hadn't really ever thought much about her daddy's leg. Yes of course she knew that he'd lost it in battle, that he had been a brave soldier fighting for his country, and she knew that he now wore a fake one, a prosthetic. It was a difficult word to say, and after Donald had stumbled over it one day and pronounced it 'pathetic', Mother had remarked that it was a very good job that Daddy wasn't at home to hear that, and we had better simply call it his 'false' leg from now on. Recalling that incident now, Martha realised just how terribly difficult it must be for Daddy to have lost his real leg, and not be able to do the physical work that he had been brought up to do. He worked in an office in London with his friend Felix who he'd met during the war, organising the transport and payment for produce between the farmers who sent it to London and the market traders who sold it.

How childish she had been until now, how innocent and oblivious. From that point on she resolved to be more considerate of Daddy, and to find a way to keep Pollywiggle Farm. She had no idea how, but she'd be on the lookout for opportunities. She would help Granny and Grandpa, she would make her family happy.

Chapter 6

Tuesday 21st December dawned bright and cold. The winter sun rose above the treetops, a hazy pale orb brightening the fields and streaking the sky pink and orange. The children were already up and sitting at the kitchen table, drinking hot sweet tea and dunking buttered toast soldiers into their boiled eggs. Granny had cut off the tops of the eggs with a knife and fanned the soldiers out around the plate with the egg cup in the middle. A little pile of salt sat on one side of the plate, in which to dip spoonfuls of egg, or pinch with your fingertips to sprinkle onto the golden yolk.

After breakfast they were planning to go back to the house in the woods. They'd woken that morning and Martha had climbed in beside Donald, so she could keep warm while she told him her plan to go back and befriend the man-who-didn't-talk, Sam. Donald was not in the least bit keen to run into the old woman again and said as much to Martha in no uncertain terms. "Mary has to leave the house sometime" she'd pointed out. "It's almost Christmas, she's going to need to visit the shops, the butchers, she'll have errands to run. I say we wait in the woods until we see her leave, then go and knock on the door. We could take Sam a piece of cake or something. We have to try to help him."

Martha always wanted to help others. "We're all put here to help others" she was fond of saying. If someone dropped money on the street, she would pick it up and run after them to give it back. If the wind snatched a newspaper out of a person's hand she would fetch it and return it. She always made sure to say hello and wave to Mr Leon who lived next door and had moved to London from Spain some years before. "Hola Senor Leon!" she would call, which made the old man smile. And once she picked up a huge May bug that had fallen from a tree onto the pavement and placed it back on a branch, despite being quite frightened by it, so that it wouldn't be stepped on. But Donald wasn't at all sure about his sister's latest good deed. "Sam doesn't talk to people Martha" he pointed out. "I don't expect he'll want to see us." "Well, we have to try" Martha retorted obstinately, and Donald knew there was no point arguing.

Now, as she was eating her egg, Martha was thinking through her plan. "Granny?" she asked. "Please could we take some fruit cake with us today for when we get hungry later?". "Well, there's not much cake left, and I was going to take some to Grandpa for his dinner" Granny replied. "But we can pack you up some sandwiches, and you can have a rock cake each if you'd like." "Yum!" said Donald "Thank you, Granny, I love your rock cakes!" "You won't be the one eating it" murmured Martha, but Donald didn't hear her, or perhaps he chose not to.

The air felt even colder than it had the previous day, and as they tramped across the frozen field, their toes grew cold inside their boots and they pulled their scarves up over their ears, and shoved hands deep into pockets. The sun wasn't breaking through the cloud cover and the woods seemed dimmer and slightly eerie, in contrast to the previous day when they had been bright and inviting. The grey sky felt oppressive as though it were a blanket weighing on the world below and muffling the light and sound of the day. The children decided to avoid going through the trees, besides they weren't entirely sure how to find the same route through that the robin had shown them. Instead, they skirted along the edge, walking the length of the field and then around the corner, where there was a track winding between the trees.

"This must be the proper way in," said Donald. "I can't see the house from here though, I think it must be pretty deep into the woods. Quite a walk yet. I'm going to need more energy, pass me my rock cake will you?"

"Oh Don" sighed Martha. "Always thinking of your tummy! We only had breakfast an hour ago, you can't make a start on your lunch already. Anyway, the rock cakes are for Sam."

"What?" exclaimed Donald, stopping in his tracks. "What do you mean? That rock cake's mine."

"I thought you realised at breakfast. I asked Granny for cake so that we have something to offer Sam. We can't just turn up on his doorstep and expect him to talk to us, we need to give him something."

"It's never going to work, this plan is stupid!" Don sulked, smarting from the thought of having to give up his rock cake. "Sam doesn't talk to anyone; he's not going to talk to you just because you give him something to eat, he's not a pet to be trained."

"He will too, you'll see! And I've brought something else as well anyway" Martha added, mysteriously.

"What? What have you brought?"

"Something you haven't thought of. Something that might get him talking. I've thought this whole thing through Don. It's NOT a 'stupid plan'."

"Stop being so secretive Martha and tell me" Donald wheedled. "I'm sorry I said it was stupid. I'm cold and was looking forward to the cake. Why don't we keep moving to warm up, and you tell me your idea as we walk?" And because she really desperately did want to share her clever idea, Martha relented. "I accept your apology" she conceded loftily, adding "And maybe we'll be able to sneak you another rock cake when we're back home again later." They set off again side by side, the argument quickly left behind, as siblings manage to do, their focus now on the shared plan.

"The other thing I've brought" Martha explained excitedly, "is piano music." She looked at Donald proudly for his reaction, but his expression was blank.

"What for?"

"Grandpa said that Sam liked to play, before the war, do you remember? "He was a great one on the piano" Grandpa said. So I've brought some music, I thought we could ask him to play for us."

"It might get him to talk to us" Donald ventured doubtfully. Secretly he didn't really understand how that would work, but he didn't want to argue again, and besides, Martha seemed so confident.

Continuing to chatter as they walked along the path, the children made their way deeper into the woods. Don pointed out mistle thrushes in the bushes and a pair of Canadian geese that were gliding overhead. As they stopped to look up at the geese, Martha became aware of another sound, becoming louder in contrast to the fading of the geese's honking. "Don!" she whispered urgently. "Footsteps!" and she grabbed her brother's hand and pulled him out of sight behind a bush at the side of the path.

Not a moment too soon. Around the bend marched Mary Ostler, her dark shawls billowing behind her like raven's wings, a black bonnet pulled low over her deeply lined face. Her footsteps crunched on the frosty track while the cane in her right hand tapped rhythmically: crunch crunch tap, crunch crunch tap. Martha and Donald crouched low behind the bush, hardly daring to breathe as she strode past. When she had disappeared from view they stood back up, stretched their legs and grinned at each other. "Perfect timing" said Martha, smiling. "You see, it's meant to be!"

Chapter 7

Picking up their pace, the children ran around the corner and saw in front of them again the red brick house at the end of the unmade road, trees surrounding it on three sides, as though being slowly enveloped by the woods. As before, the house looked dark but today there was smoke rising from the chimney. It made the place seem more welcoming and that, coupled with the fact that they knew that Mary was out, made the children feel more inclined to approach it.

Yet still Donald was hesitant. It was a stranger's house after all, and one where they may not be welcome, but Martha was already striding to the door and before Donald could voice his doubts, she had rapped loudly three times with the brass door knocker. A movement at an upstairs window caught Don's eye, and from within the house they heard the sound of slowly descending footsteps. Donald had a sudden urge to hold Martha's hand, but not wanting to seem a baby, he pushed his hands deeper into his pockets instead and took a small step backwards away from the door as his eyes darted back up the lane and his muscles tensed, ready to run. There was a rattle and a clink, and then the door opened. In front of them stood a perfectly ordinary young man, not frightening at all, looking at them inquisitively.

"Hello!" said Martha, smiling broadly. She looked and sounded confident, but inside, she was suddenly very nervous. In her head, Sam had been a teenager, he was going to be thrilled to have new friends, but now, standing on his doorstep and looking at the grown man before her, she realised that her romantic notion of helping a sad soldier wasn't the same as the reality.

Sam was in his mid-twenties, dressed in a dark polo neck sweater and trousers. His blonde hair flopped forward over his forehead and his shoulders slumped forwards too. His eyes were enquiring, but his whole demeanour was sad and dejected, and despite being a grown-up he had the air of a little lost boy about him. Martha suddenly felt rather nervous and unsure; both unusual emotions for her. "Hello" she said again, a little less certainly this time. Sam nodded in greeting, and then raised his eyebrows, and cocked his head slightly to one side, as though to ask 'can I help you?' Martha took a deep breath.

"I'm Martha Fairweather, and this is my brother Donald. We're staying with our grandparents over at Pollywiggle Farm, and we chanced upon your house yesterday. We couldn't help but notice you at the window and we thought maybe you might like some company." Sam lifted one hand to stop her there and gently shook his head as he started to close the door. "Oh! Wait!" called out Martha "Please wait! We've brought you our Granny's rock cakes. And… and…" she rummaged frantically in her bag. "Also some music for your piano. Grandpa said you liked to play. We haven't got any current music, but I've brought Grandpa's Christmas carol book, I thought you might like to borrow it." She held out the red fabric bound book and Sam took it almost automatically, the way you sometimes do when you can't help yourself accepting something being offered to you, or reaching out your hand in response to someone proffering a handshake.

With her own hands free again, Martha delved into her bag once more and found the rock cakes, wrapped in baking parchment. She held them out to Sam too.

"Please take them" she encouraged. "They're really delicious."

"They are!" piped up Donald suddenly, from behind her. He'd inched a little nearer again but was still standing close to his sister. Sam accepted the parcel and smiled at them both, looking from one to the other. He could see they meant well and he knew the Fairweathers from the farm, they were a nice family. He had noticed the children yesterday from his window, and had wondered who they were and what they were doing and was amazed that they had come back after his aunt had frightened them away like that. She was wary of people coming to the house and very protective of him. She believed that a peaceful life, away from noise and excitement, was what was best for him and he also suspected that she was worried what others would think of him.

Looking now though at the little girl and boy who had been so bold to visit him, he wondered how long it had been since he'd last seen anyone other than his aunt. His heart fluttered with a sudden anxiety, and with a final quick smile and nod of thanks he closed the door.

"Well!" exclaimed Donald. "There go our cakes."

Chapter 8

For the rest of the day, Martha couldn't settle to anything. She kept thinking of their encounter with Sam and whether it had been the right thing to do to visit him. She still firmly believed that people needed and deserved friendship, but did Sam *want* friendship, that was the question, and would he want it from a pair of children? Maybe she shouldn't have intruded. He hadn't turned them away, but he hadn't been welcoming either. And now she'd given him her grandpa's piano book and she was going to have to get it back before Christmas when Grandpa would be looking for it. Oh dear, what had she done?

She tried to distract herself with jobs on the farm. She and Donald groomed the horses, one of their favourite jobs to do. The smell in the stables was slightly sweet, warm and earthy, and the horses' breath came in bursts as they sighed and snorted in contentment. She carried felting and passed tacks to Grandpa as he mended the roof on one of the outbuildings that had blown loose in the winds, and she helped to spread fresh straw in the yard for the cattle and fill the troughs with hay.

By the time the sky began to darken she had made up her mind. She must go back to Sam, apologise for interfering and ask for the piano book back. She had made a mistake and would have to own up to it. Donald was in the house with Granny, she could see him through the kitchen window playing solitaire at the table while Granny prepared tea. 'I'll sort this out on my own' Martha thought, and setting off at a fast walk, she retraced their steps from that morning. It felt further away walking there by herself, and she started to think she should have left it until the morning, but was almost at the line of trees now and the sun was still above the woods, although slowly sinking ever lower, so she carried on.

Eventually she made it to the bend in the track, the path getting harder to see in the fading gloomy light, as the trees blocked the setting sun. She rounded the corner and there was the house. And with a sinking feeling, Martha saw Mary banging the mud off a pair of boots at the door before turning back inside and closing it behind her. Martha stood on the path, unsure of what to do next. If she waited too long Mary might see her and be angry again. If she went up to the door she could explain herself, but wasn't sure that she dared.

Suddenly, behind her, the sun found a gap in the trees on its downward course and the amber evening glow flooded through the trunks and branches to light up the windows of the red brick house. A flash of light caught Martha's eye and she turned her head, searching for the source. It was probably just the sun glinting on a pane of glass, she thought, but as she looked another flash appeared from the upstairs window, where they had first seen Sam, and then another. And another. Some were short, some long… and with a surge of excitement she realised that the flashes were intentional, that the sun was being reflected back to her, perhaps by an angled mirror. She couldn't see into the window, but Sam was communicating with her, he was using Morse code!

Martha's dad had taught them Morse code, the way to signal to others without the need for words, and she recognised it now. Dots and dashes, or dits and dahs. A dot was a quick flash, tap or tone, a dash was three times as long. She hurried to the side of the path so that she wouldn't be directly in view if Mary were to glance out, looked up at the window and began to count.

Pulling a pencil and an old paper bag from her pocket, Martha made a note of the flashes. Dash, pause, dot dot dot dot, pause, dot dash, pause, dash dot, pause, dash dot dash, pause, dot dot dot. There was a longer pause, and then the flashing began again, repeating the pattern. Martha couldn't remember the code off by heart to be able to decipher it there and then, but she was certain a message was being sent to her. And then, as quickly as it had appeared, the sun dropped behind the trees and vanished from view. The upstairs window went dark, and Martha could feel the air temperature become colder as night crept through the woods. Folding the paper bag, she placed it carefully in her pocket, then turned and ran back along the path, stumbling over roots and rocks, reaching the furrowed field just as the sun finally disappeared behind the farmhouse in the distance, and she hurried the rest of the way home in the silvery light of the risen moon.

Chapter 9

The farmhouse kitchen was warm and inviting, but the welcome was not. "Where've you bin my girl?" enquired Granny, stopping her stirring of a pan of soup on the stove to turn to Martha, her voice sharp, her face grim.

"I just went for a walk Granny. I finished my jobs and wanted to walk for a while on my own."

"We didn't know where you were!" Granny exclaimed "Off out in the dark and the cold, I've been beside myself with worry." And she sank into the chair by the range, pushing her hair back from her face which was no longer tight with anxiety and anger but collapsed into weariness with relief.

Martha hesitated by the door, not knowing how to react and feeling ashamed, both of her actions and of the lie she had told. But Granny held out her hand, and Martha gratefully walked towards this peace offering and took Granny's hand in her own. "I'm sorry" she whispered sheepishly "I didn't mean to scare you."

"What's done is done, but don't you go off in the dark on your own like that again. If you need a bit of time to yourself I understand," Granny looked at her, blue eyes searching, "but you have to let us know where you're going, and how long you'll be. Farms can be dangerous places, you know that." Martha nodded and gently squeezed her hand. "I do Granny. I really am sorry. I won't do it again."

"Right then, that's that. And now I've sat down my knees don't want me to get back up again. Give that soup a stir will you duck?"

They ate tea companionably, Grandpa telling them about the fallen tree that he had been chopping into logs that afternoon. It had come down in the winds of the week before, and now he was having to cut and clear it away, and was stacking up a good stock of firewood to see them through the rest of the winter. After tea Grandpa suggested a game of dominoes, but Martha was impatient to get Donald on his own to tell him about the secret message. She feigned tiredness and said she was going to bed early.

"C'mon Don, come up too, or you'll only wake me when you come in later."

"That's not fair! Since when do you get to tell me what to do?"

"Since forever. I'm the eldest. Bring your book and you can read in bed."

They took their hot water bottles and climbed the stairs, Donald muttering under his breath. "So bossy. It's not fair. First the rock cake, now early bed. AND you disappeared without a word."

"I have something to tell you" Martha hissed, interrupting his grumbling. "Just wait 'til you hear!" and she grinned back at him over her shoulder as she bounded up the last few steps.

In their bedroom, with the door shut, Martha quickly filled her brother in on where she had been and what she'd seen.

"I don't believe it! Let me see! I know Morse code better than you."

In the light from their candle they pored over the small

paper bag that Martha had scribbled the code on. The bag had contained ha'penny sweets which they'd eaten on the train and was now quite soft from being crumpled in Martha's pocket for two days. The pencil marks were faint, but they could make out the dots and dashes that she'd jotted down in the dim evening light.

"First a long flash, that's a 'T'" deciphered Donald. "Pass me a pencil and my notepad will you please?" He took the pad and pencil and turned to a fresh page. "T… then four short flashes, that will be an 'H'." Angling the paper bag to the light, Donald worked through the code. "It says THANKS" he concluded. "Sam was telling you 'thanks' Martha! He liked the cakes and the music. He liked us going to visit him!"

"Oh thank goodness, I was going there this evening to say sorry. I thought I'd got it all wrong, and we shouldn't have bothered him. But we were right to go Don, he must want to be friends. I'm so glad!"

In the morning the children couldn't wait to get over to the house in the woods again, but they thought they should go at the same time as the previous day. If Mary was anything like Granny, she had a certain routine, and would be going out to the shops, or for a morning walk, around the same time as before. They enjoyed a hot breakfast of porridge with some grated apple for sweetness - Granny was such a good cook - before making their way to the edge of the field where they stepped behind the solid trunk of a beech tree, and waited.

Sure enough, before too long Mary appeared from the end of the lane, her black skirts swishing. Her stride seemed less of a march today; there was a spring in her step and a carry case swung in her left hand. She turned left, away from the children's hiding spot and towards the village. They looked at each other, eyes sparkling with excitement, complicit in their adventure, and set off towards the house. As they approached, a soft melodic tinkling sound reached them, and drawing nearer they recognised it as a piano being played. "Listen Don," Martha smiled "I think Sam's playing something from Grandpa's book." As they walked up to the front door they recognised the melancholic chords of In the Bleak Mid Winter ringing out.

Donald knocked gently; abruptly the music stopped. A

few moments later the door was opened and Sam looked out at them with a shy smile, stepping back and motioning for them to come inside. Martha noticed that his smile hadn't reached his eyes. It was a start though, she thought, and she grinned back.

Chapter 10

The children followed Sam through to the parlour where he sat down at the piano and stretched his fingers over the keys, his back straightening, the red carol book open in front of him. He'd spent much of the previous evening looking through it, familiarising himself with notes and timings, discovering the music of favourite carols and working out the tune of others. Some of the carols reminded him of old times, of his mother singing along with him, and although that made him sad there was a bittersweet edge to the grief, a nostalgia of happy memories that the music evoked.

Sam had been sitting at his desk by the window in his bedroom in the evening (enjoying Mrs Fairweather's rock cakes while turning the pages of the carol book) when a movement outside caught his eye, and there he had seen Martha hesitating at the end of the lane. On the spur of the moment he'd grabbed his hand mirror and started to send the message of thanks to her by Morse

Code. He didn't know if she would understand Morse Code or if she'd be baffled by the attempt to communicate, but he made a split-second decision and in that moment was so thankful to Martha and Donald for bringing a new diversion to his life, for making contact and speaking to him. He hadn't realised how lonely he had been until he was offered a distraction to his thoughts by these brave and generous children; so kind and innocent, untouched by the horrors of war.

As he sat at the piano now Sam placed his fingers over the keys to resume In the Bleak Midwinter but then changed his mind, took the book from the music stand and held it out to Donald. Don glanced quickly at his sister, unsure that he was correctly interpreting what Sam was asking of him, but Martha nodded encouragingly and so he took the book and turned the pages.

"How about this one?" Don suggested shyly, passing it back to Sam open at 'I Saw Three Ships Come Sailing In" and Sam smiled broadly, and began to play. The jolly tempo of the familiar song filled the room, Sam's toe started tapping and the children – one either side of the piano – sang along. The carol came to an end and Sam launched straight into My Grandfather's Clock, played from memory. Donald did a little march on the spot to the rhythm, and Martha started to giggle. In response Don exaggerated his marching, adding a skip and a sway, Martha laughed even harder and all of a sudden Sam was laughing too, the sound gurgling up from deep inside, rasping against his throat and erupting from his mouth. He stopped playing, quite stunned, but the children didn't seem to register how momentous this was, and called out "Don't stop!" and "Keep playing!" through their giggles as they marched and stomped around the piano. So his fingers found the keys again, and he carried on, feeling a warmth and contentment spreading through him, a joy and unburdening of his sorrow in this moment.

Hands on automatic pilot now, Sam began another popular old song, his fingers picking out the opening bars to It's a Long Way to Tipperary without his mind consciously thinking about it. And as the melody changed his mood shifted too. Although it was an old song it had been used during the war to sing as they marched and it now held different – and not such happy – memories. His fingers faltered, slowed and stopped.

"What's the matter?" asked Donald. Sam shook his head but the children carried on looking at him quizzically, not understanding. 'It's now or never;' Sam thought to himself 'just open your mouth and speak.' He took a breath and tried to talk. "It reminds…" he began, but the words weren't coming out right. A scratchy whisper emerged, his vocal chords un-used for so long it was like starting up a rusty old piece of machinery. He cleared his throat and tried again. "It reminds me of the war" he said hoarsely.

"I'll get you a glass of water!" cried Martha, and she dashed off to the kitchen. Donald looked at Sam with concern, and then glanced away awkwardly. "Sorry" he said timidly, addressing the tiled floor, rather than looking at Sam's troubled face, "I'm sorry for what you've been through."

Chapter 11

"What did the song make you think of?" asked Martha tentatively, once Sam had sipped at the water. "Marching" Sam replied. "We marched a long, long way through France, and sang songs to keep our spirits up and our feet moving." His voice was still coming out as little more than a whisper, but it worked, he hadn't lost the ability to speak, and he found that he was glad to be talking again, strange as it felt.

"Let's sit at the kitchen table" suggested Martha. "Perhaps a warm drink would help your throat too?" Sam nodded then caught himself communicating silently, as he had done for such a long time. "Yes" he ventured, the sound of his own voice loud inside in his head. "I'll make us all a cup of tea."

Donald was not so sure that staying for longer was a good idea. He'd had a lovely morning, and was thrilled that Sam had spoken to them, but was feeling a bit twitchy that old Miss Ostler would reappear at any moment and tell them off for being there and causing so much excitement. As they followed Sam into the kitchen he nudged Martha and muttered "What about the witch? She could come back at any time!" "Oh…" Martha looked worried. "I hadn't thought of that."

Sam turned to them and smiled. "I might not have spoken for some time, but there's nothing wrong with my hearing" he said, "and the 'witch' has taken the train to visit her cousin in Cambridge for the night, so she won't be back today at all."

Donald's face turned a deep shade of beetroot. "I'm so sorry, I didn't mean to be rude."

"Don't worry" Sam reassured him, a hint of laughter around his eyes. "My aunt can be quite intimidating, I saw her chase you off the other day and I'm surprised you came back! But she's taken it upon herself to look after me and thinks the best way to do that is to keep our lives calm and quiet. She means well." Speaking again felt very strange and Sam's throat was rough and hoarse. He filled the kettle with water and placed it on the stove.

The children's curiosity about Sam was almost bubbling

out of them. Now that they knew there was no rush for them to leave, they had a hundred questions for him and wanted them all answered at once.

"How long have you been mute?" asked Don.

"What happened to you when you went missing in action?" cut in Martha. "And how did you get home again after the war, all on your own?"

"Will you live here in the middle of nowhere with your aunt forever?" exclaimed Don with a dramatic little shudder.

"Donald! Don't be so ill-mannered. And give Sam a moment to answer."

"You're the one talking over me!"

"Am not!"

"Are too!"

"How do you take your tea?" interjected Sam quietly, and the children stopped squabbling and had the grace to look slightly abashed at their behaviour.

"Milk and sugar for both of us, please" said Martha

politely.

"Sorry Sam" said Donald, sitting down. "It's just there's so much we want to ask you."

"But you don't have to answer" added Martha quickly. "It's your story, so you decide when you want to tell it and who you'd like to tell it to."

"I think I'd like to tell it to both of you" replied Sam, stirring a spoonful of honey into his tea to soothe his throat, and taking a sip. "Where shall I begin?"

Chapter 12

"I signed up to become a soldier as soon as I was 18" Sam began, "in September 1917. My dad had already been fighting for years and I wanted to get out there and help too. Help to win the war, to make things better for everyone back here, and for my dad to be back home with us again. My mum didn't want me to go but I felt that I needed to, that I should do my bit, after so many others had been out there for so long. I enlisted on my birthday, and made the solemn promise to defend the King and our country against all enemies.

I was posted to one of the new camps near Norwich to begin my basic training and the morning that I left I hugged my mum goodbye. I could see that she was holding back the tears, trying to be strong for me, and I was grateful because although I had wanted to go when it actually came to leaving I found that I was afraid. I hadn't ever spent more than a night or two away from home, and the training camp was very different to anything I had experienced before.

Over the next few months I lived in a tent, sharing with other men, all of us strangers at the beginning from different parts of the county, with different backgrounds and jobs. But now we had a common purpose, learning the routines and skills that we would need. The day started very early, with a trumpet call at 5.30 in the morning. We'd get up, tidy our quarters and have a cup of tea before heading out for the morning parade in the misty chill of the autumn dawn.

There was a lot of physical exercise in those months of training, building up our fitness, learning drills and marches, and it was a good thing too, because when we were deployed overseas we were glad of how strong and fit we had become, to manage the long marches across France. When the afternoon drill had finished, if we weren't needed for other duties, we would shine our boots and clean our kit before having some recreational time when I would write letters home and to my sweetheart Lily."

"You have a sweetheart?" interrupted Martha. "Shh Martha, let him carry on" whispered Donald, afraid that if the flow was broken Sam would stop talking.

"I had a sweetheart" replied Sam, "but she wouldn't want to know me now."

Martha opened her mouth to speak again, but Donald kicked her under the table and gave her such a ferocious glare that she closed her mouth again and remained silent, rubbing her shin and scowling at Donald.

"Back then I wrote to her though" continued Sam "and to my mum. I made friends with the other chaps and in particular a fellow named Peter. When we weren't training we'd play cards and talk about home.

There was a sense of comradeship between us all – we mostly rubbed along alright - and as time went on we were taught weapons handling, trench digging and night operations. It was hard work, but I settled into the new routine, my homesickness gradually lessened and I enjoyed learning new skills, getting fit and healthy and feeling that I was part of the war effort.

It was late on in the war when I joined up and uniforms and equipment were in short supply, but eventually I was given the full uniform and my own rifle and it was time to set off for the Front. I was sorry to say goodbye to the camp and worried about what was in store for us. I had barely even left Little Billingham before this, just once or twice to Norwich and certainly never abroad. But when we boarded the ship for France, there was such a crowd of people at the port waving and cheering us off, it made me feel proud and patriotic in my smart uniform and polished boots, setting sail to join the fighting at last, and excitement overtook the nerves.

The crossing was choppy. I felt terribly seasick as we lurched across the channel – thank goodness I hadn't joined the Navy! – and I spent most of the crossing on the deck, the cold salt spray that hit my face preferable to the stuffy air inside. Eventually we landed in France and disembarked into the spring sunshine. As new recruits we were directed first to a huge camp where new soldiers were arriving and injured soldiers returning. Seeing those men on stretchers, bandaged and bleeding, was horrifying but we had no choice but to follow orders and carry on to where we must go to fight. Marching onwards inland, towards the Western Front.

We marched for days, the sun beating down on our

backs during the day, the night temperature still cold at that time of year. We slept in billets some nights (houses where we were allowed to stay temporarily, on our way through) and made makeshift camps other nights. In the evenings when we stopped marching I took off my boots and peeled off my socks to let the air get to my blistered feet, but at first light had to pull the socks and boots back on over my raw and reddened skin to carry on marching again, putting one exhausted foot in front of the other. Left right, left right, eyes looking down at the furrows in the fields which reminded me so much of home, uncertain of what we were marching towards and when and where we would next stop.

I marched next to Peter and we kept our spirits up with the other men by singing songs and talking to distract ourselves from our increasing hunger, thirst and discomfort. When we finally reached our destination we were allowed to rest in a town a couple of miles from the front line. Kipping down in a deserted house, we spread straw on the floor and I was so tired, it felt like the most luxurious bed in the world.

Early the next morning we walked the final stretch to the

trenches, to take up our places alongside the other soldiers stationed there. Seven feet deep and six feet wide, the trenches divided the countryside in two like a great gaping wound."

Sam halted and looked at the children's young faces. He remembered how after it rained the walls and floors of the trenches turned to mud and water pooled on the ground so his feet were always wet and cold. He thought of the rats that scurried past in the dugouts while he was trying to snatch some sleep between the bouts of rapid artillery fire and earth shattering shelling. The lice that infested the soldiers' hair and uniforms, the noise and the fear and the desperate horror of seeing friends and comrades wounded, maimed, killed. The terrible long, monotonous wait for the next attack of enemy fire that turned boredom to terror in an instant. He wouldn't tell them any of this.

He simply said "I wouldn't go back there for all the money in the world."

Chapter 13

Martha looked at Sam's face, at the premature lines etched on his forehead, the sadness in his eyes. She wondered whether it had been a good idea to encourage him to talk, to remember, and yet he seemed as though now he'd started he didn't want to stop.

"What happened next Sam?" queried Donald, captivated by the story and keen to know more. "Where did you go?"

"Well," continued Sam "we held our defences for some time, advancing a little, then falling back again. We followed orders and had to trust in the greater plan, not always understanding what was being asked of us, but doing our best to hold our ground. After a couple of weeks in the trenches we would be swapped out with another battalion, returning after a short rest. It was always dreadful to have to go back to the trenches again as we were frightened and dog-tired, and never knew if that day would be our last.

Then one day, the Germans launched a fierce attack and there was a ferocious battle. We were exhausted, they overwhelmed us, and my battalion suffered dreadful casualties. We were ordered to retreat but when the order came it was too late. Peter and I heard the shout 'Fall back! Fall back!" just moments before a shell exploded right next to us. The noise was deafening. My eyes and nose were filled with dirt as a huge plume of earth was blasted into the air and I couldn't see or hear anything as I was lifted off my feet and flung to the ground where I was knocked unconscious.

When I came to, daylight was fading and the air was eerily quiet and still. There was no firing, shouting, bombs or running feet. The frantic activity of the battlefield had fallen silent and I wondered if the shell had deafened me, but there seemed to be no movement either, the field was stonily silent. Still, I was too afraid to move in case the enemy were nearby. Cautiously I opened my eyes just enough to peek through my lashes, but all I could see was soil around me, I seemed to be lying in the crater that the shell had hollowed out."

Sam thought about how he'd mentally scanned through

his body, checking his arms and legs, fingers and toes. He had ached with exhaustion and bruising, but didn't seem to be in any dreadful pain. He had been so shocked and scared though that he lay there for a very long time as the sky darkened and night fell.

The stars came out and the moon cast its ghostly light over the deserted and desecrated field. An owl hooted somewhere nearby, the only living sound in that dreadful arena of death. He had been cold, so very cold, and still dared not move, but as his fingers became numb it occurred to him that he would die there in that hole if he stayed much longer.

"Summoning all my courage, I opened my eyes again and cautiously turned my head to the side. My heart leapt as there, next to me, was Peter.

'Peter' I whispered, 'Peter!' I squinted above and around, and seeing no-one there, stiffly stretched out my arm to touch him. His hand was cold, even colder than mine, and his face, when I managed to crawl across to look at him, was vacant. He wasn't with me anymore, he had died in the blast."

Donald glanced at Martha, his face stricken, and she reached for him under the table and squeezed his hand. Sam seemed to have almost forgotten they were there. His eyes looked past them, unfocused, perhaps he was seeing that cold and silent field in his mind's eye instead of the safe, warm kitchen where they sat now.

"I think I must have entered a state of shock, because I don't remember much of what happened next. I took Peter's papers, so his family could be informed, and I must have pulled myself out of the crater and stumbled across the field. I recall seeing bodies on the ground and feeling the unnerving hush in the half dark of night. I didn't come across a single other living person, and found out later that the whole of the rest of my battalion lost their lives that day. Other units had been ordered to retreat too and the stretch of land we had been defending was now abandoned. I wandered hopelessly through the night, becoming colder and more confused, not knowing where to go or how to find where the other soldiers had retreated to. I was terrified of coming across a German brigade.

As dawn broke I made my way out of the thicket of trees

I'd been stumbling through and found myself in the town where we had spent our first night at the end of our long march. It seemed as though that had happened in a previous life and I barely recognised the place. Smoke was rising from the smouldering ruins of the church and nearby buildings and there were people on the streets, putting out fires, digging through the rubble, tending to the injured. I staggered along the road, so overcome with fatigue and despair, I no longer cared whether I was captured or not."

The air had been hazy and acrid with smoke, it caught at the back of Sam's throat and blurred his vision. Yet through the yellow mist he saw a woman piling rubble into a heap at the side of the road. She was perhaps in her early forties, slim with dark hair pinned back off her face, her strong arms lifting and stacking the fallen bricks. As Sam neared, she turned and caught sight of him, her eyes widening with surprise. Furtively she glanced around before hurrying to meet him. "A French woman saw me" Sam explained to the children. She whispered to me urgently in accented English: "Take off your jacket. The Germans are here. Quick, you must come quick with me." I slipped off my military jacket and she steered me down a side street away from the central square, away from the people and activity, towards the quiet and safety of her home."

Chapter 14

"That woman saved my life" stated Sam. He looked at Martha and Donald, coming back to the present and noticing their inquisitive expressions. "Her name was Charlotte Dubois, and she was one of the bravest people I have ever known." He drained his teacup and set it down on the table, yet still cradled it between his hands. The children sat quiet, rapt, listening to Sam whose voice was the only sound other than the occasional caw of the rooks outside and the ticking of the kitchen clock.

"The town had been occupied by the Germans, but Charlotte and her sister Clara sheltered me in their home. They risked their own lives by hiding me and keeping me safe while I recovered. I was confused and poorly for quite some time. Miraculously I hadn't been badly hurt by the blast or the firing around me, but the cold had worked itself deep into my bones and I became very ill with pneumonia, sweating and shivering in turns, unaware of where I was or the great danger the sisters were putting themselves in by protecting me. There was a cellar in their house, accessed through a trap door in the kitchen floor, and Charlotte made me a bed down there with blankets and a pillow, and concealed the entrance to the cellar so that no-one else would know that it was there.

Clara went out to work each day but Charlotte stayed home to tend the house and the garden and she brought me water and vegetable broth to sip. She placed cool flannels on my feverish forehead and sat with me when she had the time, talking in French – most of which I didn't understand - but her friendly and companionable chatter made me feel safe and I was so grateful to her.

After a few days, my temperature returned to normal, and although I was weak and tired, I felt more myself than I had in a long time. I lay on my makeshift bed, looking around the cellar at the shelves of carefully conserved produce that Charlotte must have grown and made herself. There was a tray of apples and one of pears and some knobbly yellow quinces. Two rabbits hung from a hook in the back corner of the room and jars of pickled walnuts and olives stood on the shelves.

My stomach rumbled at the thought of food, and I was just about to venture out of my bed when I heard heavy footsteps overhead.

"I do not understand French" a loud deep voice boomed, and I froze stock still, hardly daring to breathe. "If you cannot speak German perhaps you can speak English Madame Dubois?"

"A little" Charlotte's voice replied. "Would you like coffee Kapitan? Her voice was strong and sure, there was not a hint in her tone that she was frightened to have a German soldier in her house while she was hiding a fugitive.

"Nein, I would like to see your house. If you have a spare room then you must take in a German soldier to live here."

"Yes, of course" she replied. "I understand. But this is a small house with just two bedrooms, I live here with my sister and we have a room each."

"I will look" declared the soldier, and I heard his feet ascending the stairs of the little cottage, his boots ringing out on each step. My heart seemed to skip a beat with each footfall and I felt sick with fear that I was going to be discovered. "You and your sister will share a room" he called down. "There is space for a soldier to be billeted here." His boots tramped back down into the kitchen above where I lay, still propped on my elbows, my heart pounding so loudly I thought they must hear it.

"It is not perfect, but we must take what we can to keep our troops rested. A soldier will be sent here this evening, after his duties. You will make him comfortable, yes? Have his dinner ready." And with that, the man abruptly left, his footsteps moving down the hall, the front door banging shut behind him.

I heard Charlotte sit heavily into a chair and let out a long shaky breath. Finally, I could move and pulled myself up to sitting, resting my head in my hands while my breathing and heart rate returned to normal. For a few minutes there was silence. Then I heard Charlotte's chair scrape back and recognised the rustle of the rug being pulled along the kitchen floor so that the trapdoor to the cellar could be lifted open. Charlotte came down the steps and saw me watching her. "You look better Monsieur" she said. "This is good, because I must now ask you to leave. It is no longer safe for you or for me."

She went on to tell me that the British army were just a couple of miles further back, and that now I was well enough to walk, I should be able to find them. She would help me to get there. There wasn't time to form a proper plan, we had to move fast. While I dressed, Charlotte wrapped up some bread and cheese in parchment, secured with a piece of string, and filled my canister with water. She gave me a large dark jumper to pull on over the top of my uniform, both to help disguise and camouflage me. I knew that she and Clara didn't have much themselves, so her generosity and bravery was even more remarkable.

"Go out the back door" she instructed me, "and hide by the trees. I will find you." I did as I was told and moved quickly and quietly through the garden, past the apple trees and carefully tended vegetable plots, to slip unseen into the woodland. I moved back between the trees, my legs – which hadn't been used for many days - were weak and wobbly, but the air felt fresh on my face and it was good to be outside.

I heard the crunch of twigs and crouched low in the

undergrowth until I was sure that the person approaching was Charlotte. "This way" she motioned, and we hurried through the trees, away from the homely little cottage which had harboured me. We walked swiftly and silently and after a mile or so reached a river where Charlotte came to a stop. "Here, I leave you" she said. "You must cross the river and carry on, that way. Good luck to you Sam."

"I don't know how to thank you" I said, but she placed her hand on my arm to stop me from saying any more. "Stay alive" she said "that is all that I wish." And she turned and started back the way we had come, only looking back over her shoulder once to raise a hand, before disappearing between the trunks of the trees."

Chapter 15

Sam sat quietly, looking down at his cup. "I didn't ever see or hear of Charlotte again" he said softly. "I often wonder what became of her. I certainly wouldn't be here now if it hadn't been for her."

"But did you find the British army?" asked Donald. "Did you have to fight again?"

"Yes and yes" replied Sam, sighing. "They weren't so very far away. They were astonished to see me of course, and I spent a night under the surveillance of the medics because I was still so weak, but then I was set to work, thankfully back from the front line, while I recovered my strength after having been so ill.

A telegram had already been sent to my mother telling her that I was missing, presumed dead, and in all the confusion and chaos in those last months of war, and me reappearing like that to join with a new battalion, perhaps no-one ever sent another telegram informing her that I was alive after all. I wrote to her, but my letters must not have got through." Sam stopped suddenly and Martha noticed him blinking back tears before brusquely getting up from the table and turning his face away from them.

"You must be tired" she said considerately. "I expect you need a rest."

The children stood up from the table, looking at each other uncertainly. "Would you like us to leave now?" ventured Donald. "I think that might be best" said Sam, turning to look at them once more. "All this talking has worn me out, I'm not used to it." He smiled weakly. "It has been a relief to share my story though. Thank you for coming to visit me."

He suddenly looked so young and forlorn that without giving it a second thought Donald went to him and instinctively flung his arms around Sam's waist. Quite taken aback, Sam patted Donald awkwardly on the head, but the smile that grew on his face was one of happiness and affection. "You're good kids" he said gruffly. "Now get back home before your grandparents wonder what's become of you."

"We'll come again tomorrow," said Martha. "If we may."

Martha and Donald didn't stop talking all the way back to the farm, recounting Sam's story to each other, marvelling over the fact that he had spoken to them and the things he had said. Back at the farmhouse they entered the kitchen in a state of high excitement, still chattering nineteen to the dozen.

"What's all this hoo har?" exclaimed Granny, "What have you pair been doing all day long? Not up to no good I hope!"

"Oh, we have so much to tell you Granny!" cried Martha, "but we've been so busy today we missed our midday meal. Is there any chance of a sandwich while we tell you the whole story?"

"Well it's not actually long now 'til tea. If it's nothing urgent you need to tell me perhaps you could go and get yourselves cleaned up and when you come back down we'll have tea and you can tell me and Grandpa together about all your adventures."

The re-telling of Sam's story lasted over two helpings of Granny's baked egg and potato pie, and they were onto a steaming serving of apple crumble made from the autumn's harvest, before the children reached the end of their account. "Well, I'll be blowed" said Grandpa who had listened intently to the tale. "All these years he's never spoken a word, then round you two go and it's like you've opened a dam and his words have all whooshed out at once. You could knock me down with a feather." He sat back and looked at the children appreciatively, shaking his head in wonder.

"I've heard about these young men, back from the war" Grandpa continued. "I reckon young Sam has been suffering from shellshock, like so many others. The things he saw and experienced were too much for him to cope with and he's been suffering ever since. Some people say it's a sign of weakness and that those with shellshock should be carted off to the loony bin. But I don't think that's true, do you? Hearing Sam's story I don't wonder that he clammed up, trying to protect himself from his own thoughts. All that fear and fighting, and then coming back and it not being anything like the home that he left behind." Grandpa sighed sadly and Martha thought she saw his eyes glisten with unshed tears.

"That poor boy" agreed Granny. "Did you say you're seeing him again tomorrow? If Mary's away he'll be fending for himself. Bring him back here for dinner won't you? I'm sure I can rustle up enough for one more mouth to feed."

Chapter 16

Ellen had always been a good cook. Living on a farm, she and Bert grew and produced most of their food themselves, but money was always tight and so she learnt how to make the most out of the ingredients she had and how to stretch them out, using every last scrap and spoonful. Leftovers were used up in the next meal, bones boiled to make stock and broth, peelings and scraps given to the pigs and chickens and when there was a glut of fruit or vegetables in the garden Ellen pickled, preserved and conserved them to supplement their dinners in the lean winter months.

Pollywiggle had been predominately a dairy farm when Ellen moved there as a young woman to join her new husband, although they also had pigs for meat, chickens for eggs and of course a Suffolk punch to pull the plough and work the couple of fields that were given over to crops.

Ellen had thrown herself into her role as farmer's wife. She loved the routine of the farming day and the responsibility of running the house, keeping the larder stocked and the kitchen a warm and welcoming heart of the home. Most of all she loved her husband and the life they had made for themselves, working hard and enjoying the benefits of that work in being self-sufficient, companionable and content. Despite hopes for a large family they had only one child, their son Al, who was born towards the end of the old century and was the youngest in the long line of Albert Fairweathers.

Little Al was brought him up knowing the ways of the countryside and the workings of the family farm. His parents encouraged him to do his best at school, and he was as bright as a button, but the farm had to come first and so when he was needed to help out at home that's where he would be instead of in the village school house.

He grew up to be adventurous and inquisitive. He enjoyed working the farm with his father, being outside in the fresh air and endlessly occupied, yet as a young man he yearned for something more, a new challenge or a change. When he was nineteen his opportunity came. War was declared in Europe and he went straight to the enlisting station to sign up. It wasn't an obligation at the start of the war, but Al wanted to go. He said it was to protect his country but if he was truthful he also saw it as a chance for an adventure, to see some of the world and meet different people.

After waving off their only son to war, Ellen and Bert held each other tight and prayed that he would return. Ellen set to work making jams from the summer fruits: the peeling, chopping and measuring a distraction from her thoughts. Bert went out to his horse and in the privacy of the stable put his arm around the gentle mare and laid his face against her warm neck for comfort.

Managing the farm in the war years was hard physical work. Bert had lost the help of his son and also most of the men in the village who could usually be employed at busy times as they were all away at war. Over time it became increasingly difficult for food to be imported into Britain and so the government asked farmers to turn their land to arable farming to produce crops to eat including wheat for bread. Bert did his part, reducing his cattle herd to free up land for crops, and buying more Suffolk Punch horses instead to help with the increased heavy work in the fields.

At harvest time, during the long hot summer days, the corn was cut with a horse drawn binder, tied into bundles and the bundles stacked into 'shocks' like wigwams so that the corn stayed dry and the grain could continue to ripen. Ellen helped with the harvest and the Fairweathers also employed the assistance of several local women too, to stack the corn and pitch the shocks before the weather turned. They would take rest breaks perched on the back of the trailer, headscarves protecting them from the heat of the sun, swigging water from their canisters, and watching the field mice dart through the corn stalks to the safety of taller grasses where they vanished from view once more.

Letters arrived sporadically from Al who had been sent to Turkey to defend the borders there but then one day, the postboy came into the yard carrying a telegram, his face fearful and apologetic. He was only young and he hated this part of his job, being the bearer of bad news. "I'm so sorry Mrs Fairweather" he said, thrusting the letter at her as though it were burning him. Relieved to be rid of it, he turned and dashed back along the lane.

Ellen put her hand against the wall to steady herself as she looked at the telegram in her hand. "Bert" she called, her voice wavering, "Bert!" He was only across the yard seeing to the chickens, and hearing his wife call came running to her side. "Let's sit down duck" he said, leading Ellen into the kitchen and helping her into a chair. He pulled another chair alongside her and sat too, both of them now looking at the terrible missive that glowered on the table. "Best get it over with" he said, and ripped it open. Quickly scanning the contents, Bert let out his breath and grabbed Ellen in a bear hug exclaiming "He's alive!" "Oh Bert thank god, thank god" Ellen sobbed, reaching for the telegram herself where she read that Al had been badly injured in the battle of Gallipoli and was being sent home for treatment.

Chapter 17

Sam looked nervously through the back door of Pollywiggle Farm. Donald and Martha had led the way, excitedly announcing their arrival to Granny but Sam hung back a little, shy and unsure. "Come on in and sit down" Granny welcomed him kindly, holding the door open and guiding Sam through to the warm and busy kitchen. A soup simmered on the stove and Granny bustled about laying bowls and spoons on the table and directing the children. "Martha, will you pour the tea please duck? And Donald, shift Henry off that chair so Sam can sit down."

"Oh no, please don't disturb him," Sam replied quickly before falling silent once more. After talking such a lot to the children the previous day, his conversation seemed to have dried up. It was one thing recounting his story, but quite another to make small talk and conversation with other people. He felt self-conscious and bent over the chair to stroke the big ginger tom cat, so that he didn't have to talk to the others. Henry stretched languidly, turning his furry tummy up to be rubbed. A deep gravelly purr vibrated up through Sam's fingers as he stroked the contented cat.

The back door opened again letting in a rush of cold air and Grandpa entered, swiftly closing it behind him and pushing the patchwork draught excluder against the base with his foot. "How yew gettin' on boi?" he said in his broad Norfolk accent, turning to Sam and holding out his hand. "It's good to see you out and about." "I'm alright Mr Fairweather" Sam answered, "thank you."

They all sat down around the scrubbed kitchen table and Granny served up big bowlfuls of soup and dumplings. Known as 'Norfolk swimmers', Granny made dumplings that were so light and fluffy they bobbed on the surface of the soup like little boats in a harbour. Everyone tucked in and the conversation was animated as they discussed what time the children's parents would be arriving on the train the following day, the decorating of the Christmas tree, whether it was going to be a white Christmas this year and speculation as to what the King ate on Christmas Day. ("Goose of course!" exclaimed

Donald "and all the trimmings". "Or swan?" suggested Martha. "I 'spect he'll have his choice of meat, there'll have a feast laid out no doubt" was Granny's prediction.)

Sam sat quietly, watching and listening, feeling safe and contented in this happy chattering family. Occasionally he was asked for his view on something, but mostly he simply ate his soup and listened to the discussions, enjoying the companionship and connection. When lunch was finished the children asked Sam if he would like to go and meet the horses but before he could answer Grandpa said "I'd like Sam to come with me actually, if you don't mind Sam?" he turned to the young man who nodded politely. "I've got a job you could give me a hand with."

"We'll come too" said Martha, standing up, but Grandpa caught Granny's eye and she laid a restraining hand on Martha's arm. "I'd like you two to help out here please, there's bowls to wash and pans to scrub. I daresay there'll be time to show Sam the horses later on."

Sam pulled on his boots and coat, buttoning it right up to his chin against the December chill, and followed Grandpa out into the yard where he was handed a spade to carry. He wondered what they were going to do, but trusted this gentle older man and as they stomped across the field in companionable silence, he became aware of the rooks in the sky, the nature that surrounded them, and he began to relax.

Through a five barred gate and across a barren field they walked, losing sight of the farmhouse behind them, the air cold and clear as Sam breathed it in. A pair of pheasants high-stepped across the field in front of them squawking, their red heads and golden-brown plumage resplendent in the early afternoon's golden glow.

Grandpa pointed out a fallen oak tree at the boundary of one of the fields. "That's where we're headed" he stated as they walked towards it. He had already chopped off the branches and sawn off the top of the tree but the base of the big trunk still lay on its side, its roots sticking out and up into the air, looking sadly stranded and misplaced.

"I reckon we could have a go at putting her back in her hollow" said Grandpa. "Her roots are still looking strong and it's only been a couple a days that's she's been out of the ground so there's a chance if we can get her upright again she might just make a recovery. But I'm going to need your help, she's a mighty tree alright and I can't lift her on my own."

Sam nodded his agreement, laid his spade down and went round to the opposite side. Crouching low he got his shoulder underneath the heavy old trunk and on the count of three the two men heaved it up, moving the trunk steadily from their shoulders to their hands where they gave a great push and the oak up-righted itself back into the hole from which it had been ripped by the wind.

"There!" exclaimed Grandpa, satisfied. "Now we'll need to dig it in good and proper, make sure it stays in place." He and Sam picked up their spades and set to work filling in the hole and covering the roots. It was tough going as the soil had hardened with the frost of the previous day, but they persevered, unbuttoning their jackets as they worked up a sweat.

Grandpa looked across at Sam. The boy looked well, his cheeks flushed, the physical exertion and fresh air obviously doing him good. Grandpa had heard on the wireless about treatments for soldiers who had come home suffering from 'war neurosis'. One revolutionary treatment that had shown to have a positive effect on the well-being of these men was providing them with work on farms in the peace of the countryside. Therapy sessions were given alongside, and Grandpa didn't know much about that sort of thing, but the work on a farm… well that was something he could help with, something he could offer. And looking at Sam now: happy, occupied, being useful, he really believed that it would benefit the boy.

"Thass a masterous job we've made" Grandpa said, as they patted the soil around the base of the old tree and leaned on their spades. "I couldn't have done it without you Sam, thank you."

"I enjoyed it" said Sam quietly. "Is there anything else you'd like help with?"

"Well," said Grandpa, "I just so happened to be thinking about that."

Chapter 18

"Have you heard about those new American tractors Sam?" Donald asked conversationally while brushing one of the horses. "They're the cat's pyjamas! You can get 27-horsepower tractors that run on petrol. Imagine! Apparently, it only takes half an hour to plough a whole acre." He patted the big chestnut horse in front of him. "You'll be out of work" he added, addressing the horse. "If Grandpa had one of those tractors you wouldn't be pulling the plough but running around and rolling in the fields instead!"

"I have heard of them," replied Sam. He too was brushing a horse, enjoying the gentle snort and sway of their big bodies and the feeling that being next to them gave him: that of being small yet safe with these mild-mannered giants. The stable was warm and dust particles from the dry hay danced in the air.

"Mr Fairweather was telling me all about it. He says he's thinking of getting one. Thinking of taking on more help at the farm too." He paused. "He's asked me if I'd like to work here." Sam looked sideways at Donald to gauge his reaction but Donald had stopped listening at the news about the tractor.

"Grandpa's getting a tractor? That's splendid! Oh, I hope he'll let me drive it. I can't believe he's getting one!"

"Well, the farm has to move with the times. Everything's getting more industrialised and your grandpa needs more help if the farm is going to stay profitable. Also, tractors are cheaper to keep than horses."

"Oh Sam! But he'll keep the horses too won't he?"

"I 'spect so, but I don't rightly know. You'd best ask him that. Now then," said Sam, laying down the brush and giving his horse a last long stroke and a pat on her elegant neck. "I need to get back before Aunt Mary gets home and finds the house empty. I have a lot to tell her."

"Ok Sam. We'll see you in the morning then, do you still want to come into the town with us tomorrow, for some last-minute Christmas shopping?"

"Yes I will do, I think it's about time I showed my face

again, and I reckon I can do it with you and Martha by my side."

"See you then. Mind how you go."

Sam smiled at Don as he passed him, letting the stable door swing shut as he stepped out into the cold white afternoon. His head was spinning with all that he had done, said, seen and learnt over the last couple of days. Had it really only been two days? He felt as though his life had been kickstarted again, and he was ready for it to happen. Mr Fairweather had offered him a position on the farm, helping Jack the farmhand with odd jobs and also working closely with the old man himself, learning the trade.

He was looking forward to seeing Aunt Mary when she returned home from her visit. Looking forward to talking to her and letting her know that her care and protection of him over the last few years had helped him to reach this point where he felt he was ready to join the world again. It was all going to come as quite a shock to her, so he'd better get back and get the kettle on the boil ready to make her a hot sweet tea while he told her the events of the previous days. He quickened his pace and hastened home to the little house in the woods, his mind whirring, hope in his heart.

Chapter 19

Christmas Eve, and the market town of Little Billingham was a flurry of activity. Families strolled together along the streets, sharing season's greetings with people they knew, arms laden with boxes and parcels. The shop windows were invitingly lit from within and displayed enticing arrays of food, toys and treats while the scent of warm gingerbread wafted down the high street from the bakery's open door. Market traders called out their prices and wares, and there was a buzz of excitement in the air as busy shoppers checked their lists to make sure they had all the fresh food and final gifts needed for the following day.

A queue had formed outside the butchers as customers waited patiently to pick up their Christmas meat orders. Those who had already been served exited the shop encumbered with large parcels of meat and pies wrapped securely in brown paper and string, and purposely set off on their next shopping mission. 'C.P. Nathan and Sons,

Local Butchers' announced the sign above the shopfront, and the name was also inscribed on the large picture window in which braces of pheasants and rabbits were hung and trays showcased veal pies, pink hams, and glazed ox tongue.

Martha, Donald and Sam stood in the queue, waiting their turn. "What is it you're collecting?" asked Sam. "Goose" replied Martha. "A big one! More than enough for the six of us, I 'spect we'll be eating it for the next week!"

"What are you picking up Sam?" enquired Don.

"A pheasant. That's what Mary always likes to have. When I was younger we used to have a couple of rabbits. My dad would often catch them himself and mum would roast them for our Christmas dinner." Sam's face took on a far-away look as he remembered times past.

"What else did you do on Christmas Day? We have stockings in the morning, then church, then finally presents after lunch. It's such a long time to wait!" moaned Don.

"Same" said Sam. "I remember the dinner going on and

on when I was a boy and wanting to get to my presents! The grown-ups liked to sit and chat, take their time. And then, just when you think it's finally finished, there's all the clearing of the table and the washing up to do!"

"That's EXACTLY what happens with us too!" agreed Martha indignantly.

"After the presents we would sit around the table and play games" Sam continued. "Perhaps a new game we'd got as a gift, but most usually cards. My mum loved playing cards. Rummy, Whist, Sevens, it didn't matter what it was, but she was competitive!" He laughed "She wasn't a graceful loser. Or a graceful winner come to that! And then we'd play the piano and sing songs and if I was the one playing then my mum and dad would dance together." Sam's smile became wistful.

"You know the lovely thing about memories?" Martha said, looking up at Sam. "They're with you forever, you can remember them whenever you like. But you can also make new memories to add to the bank in your mind, so in the future you have even more lovely things to look back on."

"Who made you so wise?" joked Sam, but he smiled as he thought how right she was.

They had reached the front of the queue, and Donald went up to the butcher's counter to ask for their Christmas goose. "There you go young master Fairweather" said the butcher as he handed over a large parcel. A ruddy-faced young man, his shirt sleeves were rolled up exposing powerful forearms and big hands that efficiently selected, cleaved and sliced the meat before wrapping it in paper. No older than his mid-twenties, he must have been one of the sons of Nathan and Sons. "Your Granny's already settled up with me, so there's nothing to pay today. Have a very happy Christmas now and tell your Granny and Grandpa I said hello won't you?" He wiped his hands on the red and white striped apron tied around his waist and turned to serve the next customer. "Next!" he called as Donald moved away and Sam stepped forward. "Sam Butters?" the butcher's eyes widened in surprise as he did an almost comical double take. "Well, I'll be beggared."

Chapter 20

Sam smiled nervously. "Hello Josh" he said. He and Josh Nathan had been at school together, but he hadn't seen him now for many years. "It is you!" replied the butcher, coming out from behind his counter. "It's good to see you" he said sincerely, shaking Sam's hand with one of his and grasping him on the shoulder with the other. "I didn't know if I'd ever see you out and about again."

"First time out in a long time" replied Sam shyly, flattered by the reaction.

"Well I'm pleased as punch" said Josh, giving Sam one last pat and an understanding smile. "Now then" he continued briskly, moving back behind the counter. "Are you picking something up this morning?"

"Yes, a pheasant please, Miss Ostler would have ordered it."

Josh turned to fetch the pheasant and handed the parcel to Sam. "There you go Sam Butters. Sam Butters!" he repeated, as if he couldn't quite believe it. "This one's on us." "Oh no – " started Sam "I couldn't - ", but Josh shook his head. "Git orn with you" he said. "Enjoy that pheasant, and have a very merry Christmas. We'll see you again before too long I hope." He waved away the money that Sam was holding out to him and turned to the next customer. "Thank you" said Sam "Thank you so much" and he wasn't just talking about the pheasant. The whole encounter had made him feel wanted and welcomed, and a warmth spread through him despite the frost on the pavement and the chill in the air. "Come on Sam!" called Donald "There's still lots more we need to do!"

The next stop was the grocers for a tin of savoury biscuits, some stilton and cheddar cheese, and a little box of sugar plums. The children gazed at the displays of tins of biscuits, treats and stacks of dried fruits, sugar and spices. The next shop window was filled with tree crackers and candles, hanging paper honeycomb decorations and rocking horse and Nutcracker ornaments to adorn Christmas trees. As the three of them walked through the streets occasionally someone recognised Sam and nudged their neighbour, or (more politely) nodded and smiled at them. The happily festive mood was infectious and Martha found herself walking along with a bounce in her step.

At the toy shop they slowed down to peer at the delights inside. Train tracks were set up so that the electric trains looped around the display, through tunnels and past piles of gift-wrapped parcels. Further back in the shop were bicycles, drums, dolls and hand-painted tin ships which could be sailed on the pond. "Let's go inside" begged Donald, "just to look. Please?"

The door opened with a tinkle and Donald and Martha rushed straight to the window display to look at the trains up close. Sam wandered into the shop, marvelling at all the toys available. Suddenly, the hairs on his arms pricked up and he had the feeling that someone was watching him. He turned to look. A young woman stood nearby, clutching her shopping bag to her chest and gazing at him as though he was a rare wild bird that she was trying not to startle.

"It is you" she said in a whisper. "Imogen just told me she'd seen you walking down the street but I didn't believe her." She put her hand to her mouth. "Oh Sam" she said in a choked voice, her eyes filling with tears, "I am glad to see you." Sam stood stock still, taking in the sight of her familiar face, now just a little older, sadder, thinner than he remembered. "Lily" he said, and a complex mix of emotions rose within him: happiness to see her yet sorrow for the time lost, hope that she may want to talk to him but regret at not having started speaking again earlier. "It's been so very long."

"I called on you several times when I first heard you were back, but Aunt Mary always told me you were too unwell for visitors. Over time I learnt that you didn't speak to anyone any more and in the end I resigned myself to the fact that you wanted to be left alone, or were too ill to see me."

"I'm sorry Lily" said Sam helplessly. "I *was* ill, Aunt Mary was right. But I think things are starting to get better again now."

"Sam! Sam!" Donald called from the other side of the room. "You've got to come and see these trains, they're splendiferous!"

Lily looked at him questioningly. "The Fairweather kids"

he explained, adding proudly "I'm going to be working at Pollywiggle Farm."

"That's wonderful Sam, really wonderful! Perhaps… would you like to tell me all about it over a cup of tea sometime?"

"I'd like that very much."

"Sam! SAM! Come and SEE!"

He smiled apologetically at Lily and she grinned back. "Sounds as though you're in demand" she said. "Let me know about that cup of tea, and have a merry Christmas. It really is so very lovely to see you." She turned at the door to smile back at him again and he felt his cheeks flush and his heart give a little flutter. As he walked towards the children Martha noticed that now his smile was genuine and that this time the joy reached right to his eyes.

Chapter 21

Grandpa had sawn a little bushy pine tree from the edge of the woods, brought it to the farmhouse on the back of the cart and heaved it into the house, leaving a trail of pine needles in his wake. Granny was sweeping up the needles while Grandpa wedged the tree upright in a bucket when the children returned from town with all the food for Christmas dinner.

"Thass on the huh" said Granny, leaning on her broom and appraising the wonky looking tree from the other side of the room.

"Give me a minute Missus! I'm gettin' these stones in here to stand it straight."

"It's a beauty Grandpa!" Martha remarked. "We'll get these things away and then come and help."

"I'll sort out the food" said Granny, coming to look in the boxes and bags. "Thank you, you two, for fetching all this. You give Grandpa a hand and look in them boxes there for the decorations and such like, while I make a start on the mince pies. Your parents will be arriving before too long, and it would be nice to have the place all festive for when they get here."

Once the tree was standing proudly perpendicular Martha and Donald carefully took out the delicate glass Christmas baubles from their box, each one individually wrapped in newspaper from when they had been packed away the previous year. They uncovered striped baubles, gold ones, turquoise with gold edging, pink with silver swirls, and their favourite, a long teardrop shaped ornament painted pale green with intricate white feather patterns. All were hung upon the tree and then the foil lametta, looking like tiny icicles, was draped over the branches so that the whole tree sparkled and twinkled. Grandpa attached candles to the ends of the branches, ready to light later, and then they turned their attention to the rest of the decorations.

Lengths of ivy, cut from the trees in the wood where they had wound their tight tentacles into the bark, were strung along the top of the hall walls and criss-crossed the ceiling. Paper chains were deftly mended where they had come apart and looped from corner to corner to dress the drawing room. Sprigs of freshly picked glossy green holly leaves, some with scarlet bright berries, were perched above pictures and mirrors, and paper snowflakes were hung from ribbons on the walls.

By the time the decorations were up they were all in need of a break. Granny had made the mince pies and fresh bread was proving on the top of the range. "Let's have a nice cup of tea" she said "then maybe Martha, you could help me with getting the vegetables prepared ready for tomorrow. Thass a rare great goose you picked up today, we've food enough to see us through to next Christmas!" she joked.

"I've an idea" said Grandpa, leaning back in his chair, his big hands crossed contentedly over his stomach. He looked at his happy, helpful grandchildren, his hard working and generous wife and the large Christmas cake on the work surface waiting to be iced, and he felt grateful and full of Christmas spirit. "Why don't we see if Mary Ostler and Sam would like to join us for Christmas dinner? It ent much of a celebration with just the two of them out at that little house and as Granny said, we've enough food to sink a ship."

"Oh Grandpa, what a wonderful thing to suggest!" cried Martha. "Can we Granny?" chimed in Donald, then remembering their last encounter with Sam's aunt, adding "Oh, I'm not sure about Miss Ostler though, she might still be cross with us and not want to come."

"She didn't know you before" said Granny, "but Sam will have told her all about you now and I 'spect she'll be very happy to get to know you better. She's a good woman Donald, she was just looking out for Sam, that's all. Give her another chance and she'll give you another one too."

"As to having them over for Christmas" Granny continued, "well, I reckon that there's a grand plan" and she went to sit beside Grandpa and put her hand on his knee. He placed his own big calloused hand over hers and gave it a squeeze. The kitchen smelt delicious and a soothing warm cup of tea was just the ticket after all the activity of the day. Henry the marmalade cat stretched and yawned on his range-side throne. The family sat back in their chairs and admired their handiwork: the tree, the decorations, the food preparations, and they felt like the luckiest people in the world.

Chapter 22

The fire in the drawing room grate crackled and the candlelight from the Christmas tree bathed the room in a soft yellow glow. Al and Emily had arrived by train in the late afternoon and were delighted to be reunited with their children. They carried in armfuls of presents, wrapped in paper that had been printed with green holly sprigs, and Donald arranged them under the tree with the parcels already under there.

Now, having had supper, they all sat around the fire reaching their toes towards the warmth in the grate; the golden glow and gentle flickering of the flames were calm and comforting. The adults had a small glass of sherry each and there were mugs of cocoa for the children.

"Tell me more about this tractor you're thinking of getting then Pa" said Al "Don's told me they're mighty powerful."

"That they are" Bert replied "They'd git the job done in half the time, and when they're not being used you don't hafta pay to keep them like you do horses; just the fuel that you use of course. It's a big outlay to get one to start with but I've been thinking a lot about it and it makes sense in the long run, what with the efficiency of the machine."

He looked at his son and thought how good it was to have him home and that this might be as good a time as any to broach his idea.

"Now" he started, "hear me out here boy. I ent zackly sure if this would work, but I've been looking at how you get in and out of these tractors, and I know you could get up into them with a hop and a skip no bother. Then driving it, well, that's what I'm not hoolly certain of, but it looks to me as though you could do that too. It's definitely a better prospect than you walking along the uneven furrows behind the horses, what with your leg, and so I was thinking - me and your ma were thinking – maybe you might like to give it a try."

Al looked at him thoughtfully and opened his mouth to speak, but Grandpa quickly carried on.

"Now, before you start telling me you can't do lots of the other things on the farm, I've got a proposition for you. I know that Donald and Martha here have filled you in on the story of them befriending young Sam Butters, and that he came the other day to help me out with a few jobs. He's a quick learner, a nice lad, and he's keen to work. It'll do him the world of good working here, I reckon.

So p'raps, you might like to have a think about how it would be to drive the tractor and manage the farm, and have Sam - and also Jack of course - working for you. I'm gettin' on a bit now son, and am going to need to take a step back from the heavy work soon."

Grandpa stopped talking and took a sip of his sherry. Al and Emily looked at each other.

"That's a lot to think about" said Al, slowly. "I'd have to actually go to try out a tractor of course to see if I could operate it. And Emily and I would need to discuss it together. We'd all need to discuss it, the whole the family" he added as he noticed Donald and Martha gazing at him, their eyes shining and hopeful.

Emily spoke up. "If things work out with Sam we might be able to get word out to other war veterans who would benefit from some outdoor work too" she suggested. "If it helps them and also helps us, it's worth finding out more about it, isn't it?"

The adults talked enthusiastically about therapy for shell shock, about the benefits of farm work, about how much Al would like to be back working on the farm too, about the impressive new machines that could help with the work.

Suddenly, Donald yawned loudly and Martha poked him "Shh!" she hissed and he covered his mouth with his hand, trying to stifle the sound, but it was too late. Their parents had heard the yawn and said that it was time for bed. "Remember your stockings!" said Granny, holding out two of Grandpa's long winter socks. "Lay them over the end of your beds and we'll see if Father Christmas comes in the night."

"I'm going to stay awake all night so that I see him" announced Donald, but of course he didn't. Tucked into their cosy beds with hot water bottles at their feet and kisses from their parents, it wasn't long before tiredness took over. Despite the excitement they felt at the possibility of moving to Norfolk and all the things they wanted to talk to each other about, before they knew it they were both fast asleep.

Chapter 23

The disappointment of missing Father Christmas visiting in the night barely even registered the next morning, as Martha's eyes lit upon the big sock tied around her bedpost, bulging with gifts. "Don! Don!" she cried "It's Christmas! Happy Christmas Don!" she grabbed her stocking and jumped into bed with her brother who was wriggling himself up to a seated position and rubbing his eyes. He caught sight of his stocking too and turned to Martha, his eyes gleaming. "Let's take them through to Ma and Pa's to open them. Come on Martha!"

In bed with their sleepy parents, the children pulled the presents out of their stockings one by one. Bags of nuts, candy canes and shiny new pennies emerged from the depths of the socks, followed by a sharp new pencil for Martha and a smooth blue marble for Donald with white swirls that looked like clouds on a summer's day. At the toe of each stocking was a beautifully crisp apple, polished to a shine that gleamed in the candlelight of the still-dark morning.

Once dressed and breakfasted the family walked together to church, crunching through the snow that had fallen in the night. A muffled hush lay over the village and the lane from the farmhouse was so peaceful, the countryside so beautiful, and the day so very special, that the family were reverentially quiet as they walked along the farm lanes taking in the wonder of the natural world around them.

As they approached the church the chatter of other families reached them and soon they were greeting friends and neighbours and exchanging Christmas wishes as they filed into the church pews. The end of the pews had been decorated with arrangements of holly and ivy, and the church was filled with people of all ages wearing their best Christmas clothes, brightening the dim interior with colourful hats and scarves, the children's mother in her red coat looking particularly festive.

They spotted Mary and Sam near the front and waved. And Martha noticed Lily across the aisle, dressed warmly with her hands encased in a muff, casting a quick glance at Sam. Little children whispered to each other throughout the service, some of them impatiently wriggling in their seats, and while some of the prayers and the sermon did seem to go on (to Martha and Donald, who were keen to get back home), the carols were joyful and uplifting. Sung with such enthusiasm, the range of voices rose and fell, reaching the rafters and lifting the spirits; from Grandpa's deep bass voice booming out the familiar words, to the soprano voice of Freya Beaumont, Little Billingham's best singer (who everyone said should be on the stage). Her clear tones soared above the others as she reached the heights of the descant part to the final verse of O Come All Ye Faithful and brought the more sentimental members of the congregation to tears.

The children looked at each other and beamed. They loved these Christmas traditions and experiences; the wonderful predictability, the same carols sung, the same faces and voices, the same routine to the day. Next would come lunch, then presents, then games and perhaps some songs at the piano. But this year there would be something different. This year there would also be Sam.

Chapter 24

Outside the church, Mary and Sam found the Fairweathers waiting under one of the huge yew trees calling 'Goodbye!" and "Merry Christmas!" as people passed them. They all set off for the farmhouse together, tramping through the snow. "Come along!" called Granny "I need to check on the goose and get the rest of the dinner on" and she led the way at a fast pace, the others following behind, chatting excitedly about the food, presents and treats to come.

Granny's Christmas spread that year surpassed even previous festive feasts: succulent goose and crispy roast potatoes, sprouts, cabbage, parsnips and carrots that had all been grown on the farm, and a rich dark gravy to accompany it. The main course was followed by a juicy figgy pudding, heavy with fruit and served with fresh warm custard. While everyone tucked into the food, talk turned again to the topic on everyone's minds: the future of the farm.

"Emily and I had a good long talk last night" began Al. "If I can use these new tractors and if the children are in agreement" here he looked at Martha and Donald, who were already nodding furiously, wide eyed with excitement, anticipating what was coming next, "then we would very much like to come to live and work on the farm."

"There's an awful lot to consider though" he added firmly, halting the children mid-cheer, "including whether Sam would like to work with us and not least the practical matter of how all the family would comfortably live here together."

"Well we would move out of the farmhouse to the little workers' cottage down the lane" answered Granny. "Jack no longer uses it, he has a house in the village now where he and his wife chose to live when they got married, so the cottage is empty and would suit us perfectly. Grandpa and I have already discussed this and think it would be just right for us. Close to the farm and all of you, but our own little space all the same."

Then Sam spoke up. Although his voice was soft, everyone turned to look at him and listen. "I can't think of a better place to work than here" he said. "Meeting Martha and Donald was one of the best things that has ever happened to me. To be back amongst other folk again, a good job offered to me, new friends around me… and my home to return to each night" – he smiled at his aunt, who patted his hand and smiled back – "I couldn't have wished for more this Christmas."

Granny turned to the children and gave a wink. "I reckon you can carry on with that cheering now ducks" she said and looking round the table, raised her glass. "Hurray!" Donald shouted. "Hurray!" everyone answered, laughing. "Merry Christmas!"

After lunch the children were desperate to get to the presents, but the grown-ups seemed in no hurry. The dinner plates were cleared but then the dishes needed to be washed and put away, the table wiped, the floor swept, and just when Donald thought there couldn't be anything else left to do, Grandpa suggested a nice cup of tea and Granny went off to put the kettle on. Eventually, with everyone settled in armchairs with cups of tea it was finally time to open the presents.

The children gifted cloth peg dolls that they had made,

and poems and pictures they'd written and drawn. Hand knitted socks and gloves emerged from the parcels from Granny and Grandpa, and deliciously sweet crumbly fudge was given by Mary who had turned out not to be the least bit scary after all! She was fiercely protective of her nephew, that much was clear, but once she had seen how happy Sam was in the company of the Fairweathers she had softened and sat now with a teacup in her hand, watching the presents being opened, with a smile on her face that was as sweet as her fudge.

Donald loved the stamp album from his parents, but secretly his favourite gift was from Sam: a spinning top striped with green, red and gold which all merged together as it twirled and twisted across the floor. Martha with thrilled with a skipping rope with smooth wooden handles and from her parents a forest green scarf made from the softest wool and a rag doll that she immediately named Mia, after a glamorous actress she had heard of. Surrounded by presents and paper, she looked around at her family and their new friends, and felt very fortunate indeed.

Chapter 25

Grandpa was dozing in the armchair by the fire and the children were playing cards on the hearth rug when Granny came in carrying a tea tray. "I couldn't eat another mouthful!" protested Emily, but at the sight of cheese and biscuits, homemade pickles and green tomato chutney, gingerbread and mince pies, it was surprising how peckish everyone found themselves after all.

"No more snoozing!" cried Granny as Grandpa settled comfortably back into his chair. "We've become soporific from all the food and warmth. Up you get, all of you! Time for some music I think, to wake us all up. It's still Christmas Day after all! Sam, would you do the honours?" Sam didn't need to be asked twice. He sat down at the piano and opened Grandpa's red book which he'd brought along with him.

The family gathered around the piano to sing as Sam played Good King Wenceslas. Martha hung back, straightening up the deck of cards in her hands, watching the happy faces and noticing the ease with which Sam and Mary had been accepted into the family. She felt as though she had grown up over the last few days and was no longer a little girl, that something had shifted inside her, something had changed. She had learnt a little of what Sam – and all those other men - had been through and also now understood the hardships and difficulties that her own family had been grappling with. She felt proud that she'd been part of finding a way for the family business to continue and for her dad to be able to live and work on the farm again. What a lot had happened in the last week and what a lot more lay ahead for their new life in Norfolk.

She put down the cards and in doing so caught sight of her new doll. She may be growing up but she wasn't too old for a doll yet she thought as she picked Mia up and went to join the others at the piano. They had finished Good King Wenceslas and were singing It Came Upon the Midnight Clear. Donald slipped his hand in Martha's and whispered "This is what the carol singers sang on our first night here, do you remember? It seems such an age ago." Martha squeezed his hand and said playfully "A week really is a long time for a little squirt like you" and they jostled each other good humouredly as Grandpa's deep voice filled the room with the final words of the carol:

"And man at war with man hears not, The tidings which they bring, O hush the noise, ye men of strife, And hear the angels sing."

THE END

ABOUT THE AUTHOR

Jane Swift grew up in Norfolk but has lived in Cornwall for the last twenty years. She lives by the sea with her husband and two children.
The Silent Soldier is her first novel.

Printed in Great Britain
by Amazon